Novels for Students, Volume 30

Project Editor: Sara Constantakis Rights Acquisition and Management: Leitha Etheridge-Sims, Sari Gordon, Aja Perales, Jhanay Williams Composition: Evi Abou-El-Seoud Manufacturing: Drew Kalasky

Imaging: John Watkins

Product Design: Pamela A. E. Galbreath, Jennifer Wahi Content Conversion: Katrina Coach Product Manager: Meggin Condino © 2010 Gale, Cengage Learning

For product information and technology assistance, contact us at **Gale Customer Support, 1-800-877-4253.**

For permission to use material from this text or product, submit all requests online at **www.cengage.com/permissions.**

Further permissions questions can be emailed to **permissionrequest@cengage.com** While every effort has been made to ensure the reliability of the information presented in this publication, Gale, a part of Cengage Learning, does not guarantee the accuracy of the data contained herein. Gale accepts no payment for listing; and inclusion in the publication of any organization, agency, institution, publication, service, or individual does not imply endorsement of the editors or publisher. Errors brought to the attention of the publisher and verified to the satisfaction of the publisher will be corrected in future editions.

Gale
27500 Drake Rd.
Farmington Hills, MI, 48331-3535

ISBN-13: 978-0-7876-8687-1
ISBN-10: 0-7876-8687-5
ISSN 1094-3552

This title is also available as an e-book.
ISBN-13: 978-1-4144-4946-3

ISBN-10: 1-4144-4946-1

Contact your Gale, a part of Cengage Learning sales representative for ordering information.

Printed in the United States of America
1 2 3 4 5 6 7 13 12 11 10 09

Around the World in Eighty Days

Jules Verne 1872-1873

Introduction

Titled *Le tour du monde en quatre-vingts jours* in
the original French, *Around the World in Eighty
Days* is perhaps the best known of Jules Verne's
novels, especially through its film adaptations.
Verne authored one of the first literary "franchises,"
with his works marketed to maximum profit
through the use of the new mass media, and *Around
the World in Eighty Days* first appeared in serial
form in the French newspaper (owned by Verne's
book publisher) *Le Temps* (*The Times*). The first

installment was published on December 22, 1872, which is also the dramatic date of the closing of the novel. This led to the misconception that the story was reporting actual events. In any case, journalists lost no time in replicating the voyage around the world as the basis of popular news stories and continued to do so through the twentieth century, most recently in Michael Palin's 1988 British Broadcasting Corporation (BBC) series, as the idea of such a journey became part of modern mythology.

Around the World in Eighty Days is somewhat unusual among Verne's work, or at least among his works that are best known today. Verne helped to create the genre of science fiction, and many of his novels either concern a voyage of fantastic scientific discovery (*Cinq semaines en ballon* [*Five Weeks in a Balloon*], 1863; *De la Terre à la Lune* [*From the Earth to the Moon*], 1865) or imagine the ramifications of technology that did not yet exist but seemed likely to be developed in the near future (*Vingt mille lieues sous les mers* [*Twenty Thousand Leagues under the Sea*], 1869-70). *Around the World in Eighty Days*, however, deals only with exploiting existing technology, especially railways and steamships, to its limits. The novel celebrates the nineteenth-century idea of progress, the concept that life was being constantly improved by new technological advances. For the details of the plot, Verne drew on a series of newspaper articles and journalistic books touting that, according to the schedules of transportation companies, a voyage around the world in eighty days should be possible, so the book's premise is not fantastic as much as enthusiastic about what technology had already achieved.

Author Biography

Jules Gabriel Verne was born on February 8, 1828, in the city of Nantes, a prosperous port on the Atlantic coast of France. His father was a successful lawyer, and Verne received a classical education at Saint Donatien College (a Catholic boarding school). In 1847 Verne began to study law in Paris (completing his degree by 1849), but he also began to write for the theater, and it was this second career that increasingly interested him. In 1852 there was a definitive break with his family when Verne refused to take over his father's law firm in Nantes. Verne was eventually forced to work as a stockbroker to support himself and the new family he acquired in 1857 when he married Honorine de Viane, a widow with two children.

In 1862 Verne began to work with the publisher Pierre-Jules Hetzel. By 1864 Verne was writing novels full-time and had become an unprecedented literary success. His works, beginning with *Cinq semaines en ballon* (*Five Weeks in a Balloon*, 1863), were serialized in Hetzel's magazines and then republished in book form. Hetzel created a special series for Verne's novels, Voyages extraordinaires. In part because of Hetzel's marketing genius, all of Verne's books were financial successes. His novels were always tales of fantastic adventure, and while most merely took place in exotic locales, many engaged directly with the fact that technology and industry were changing the conditions of life in France (and in western Europe and the United States) at an ever-increasing rate. They frequently dealt with technological developments or discoveries that had not yet occurred (or at least had not yet been fully exploited) but which seemed inevitable. These included such ideas as aerial warfare (*Robur-le-conquérant* [*Robur the Conqueror*], 1886) and manned exploration of the moon (*De la Terre à la Lune* [*From the Earth to the Moon*], 1865). Others reinterpreted traditional mythological themes, such as the existence of an underworld below the surface of the earth, in a scientific style (*Voyage au centre de la Terre* [*Journey to the Center of the Earth*], 1864).

Around the World in Eighty Days (1872-73), on the other hand, was drawn from journalistic promotion that such a journey, unthinkable in Verne's youth, had become possible because the world had been linked together by a network of steamships and railways. Far from being a prediction of future achievement, it was a celebration of the technological progress that the nineteenth century had already witnessed. The optimistic tone of the novel was well received in France, a nation that had just had its confidence badly shaken through defeat in the Franco-Prussian War (1870-71). Verne and Hetzel badly needed a new financial success after the loss of income occasioned by the war and a nearly four-year cessation in publishing. As Verne's first new book after this period, *Around the World in Eighty Days* did not disappoint, becoming one of the pair's most successful enterprises, especially owing to sales in England, where the nationality of the protagonist Phileas Fogg contributed to its popularity.

Verne thus resumed his career as author of one of the most popular literary franchises in the world, publishing novels until 1897 (*Le sphinx des glaces* [*An Antarctic Mystery: The Sphinx of the Ice Fields*]). Verne published sixty-four novels in all in his lifetime. After Verne's death, Michel Verne completed several of his father's unfinished manuscripts, also published by Hetzel's company through 1919. In 1888 Verne was elected to the city council in Amiens, and he enjoyed a minor career in local politics. Verne died on March 24, 1905, of a sudden onset of diabetes (then untreatable) in his adopted home in Amiens.

Chapters 1-4

Verne begins *Around the World in Eighty Days* with descriptions of his two main characters, the mysterious gentleman Phileas Fogg and his newly hired manservant Passepartout. Fogg is said to keep to a mechanically precise daily schedule, being occupied each day with going to and from the Reform Club (a prestigious association that catered to the British elite), where he took his meals, read several newspapers, and played the card game whist in the evening before returning home. One evening, Fogg overhears two bits of news that will drive the plot of the novel. The first is that the Bank of England was robbed of fifty-five thousand pounds, and the police are watching all ports of exit from the country for the thief, on the premise that he will flee, and have even sent detectives off to transportation hubs around the world to watch for him. A reward of two thousand pounds and five percent of any money recovered has been offered to these officers. One of Fogg's whist partners suggests that the thief will not be caught because the world is too large to search. Fogg takes exception to this and insists that it is being made smaller by the new steam transportation network.

Media Adaptations

- *Around the World in Eighty Days* (1874) is a stage play by Verne and Adolphe d'Ennery based on working drafts of the novel; a special-effects extravaganza, it was frequently produced in Paris through the 1950s.

- In 1919 a German satirical version of *Around the World in Eighty Days* was directed by Richard Oswald. All prints of this film have been lost, however.

- An Academy Award-winning film of *Around the World in Eighty Days* was directed in 1956 by Michael Anderson, starring David Niven; it was produced by the Michael Todd Company and released by United Artists.

- In 1963 the novel was again satirized in *The Three Stooges Go Around the World in a Daze*, directed by Norman Maurer for Columbia Pictures and starring Moe Howard, Larry Fine, and Joe DeRita.

- In 1989 a television miniseries of *Around the World in Eighty Days*, directed by Buzz Kulik and staring Pierce Brosnan, Eric Idle, and Peter Ustinov, was syndicated to various European television networks.

- Also produced in 1989, Michael Palin's BBC documentary *Around the World in Eighty Days* retraced the route of the journey in the book.

- In 2001 the playwright Mark Brown staged a new adaptation of *Around the World in Eighty Days*.

- In 2004 a loose adaptation of *Around the World in Eighty Days* was directed by Frank Coraci for Walt Disney Pictures and starred Jackie Chan.

Another acquaintance introduces the other point, a newspaper article suggesting that, with the unification of the railway network in India, a journey around the world could be completed in eighty days. Fogg takes up this notion and eventually proposes to undertake such a journey. Wagers are quickly made with several club members over whether he can complete the journey. These bets amount to twenty thousand pounds (a sum equal to at least two million dollars in today's money), half of Fogg's total fortune. Fogg leaves immediately with an incredulous Passepartout on the overnight train-boat service heading for Dover (the regular service between London and Paris on which passengers traveled on a train, switched to a boat across the English Channel, and finally transferred to a second train to reach the opposite city, all on a single ticket).

The introductory chapters foreshadow a motif that is occasionally alluded to throughout the work and which accounts for the final turn of the plot. Fogg asks Passepartout the time, and when the manservant replies that it is 11:22 Fogg tells him that his watch is four minutes slow. Passepartout denies that this is possible since his is a very good watch, of which he is notably proud, that does not lose time. However, four minutes is the difference between the true local times of London and Paris, where the watch was presumably originally set. Periodically throughout the novel, the fact is mentioned that Passepartout keeps his watch on London time (as he thinks) and so becomes increasingly out of synch with the local time as the journey proceeds. The narrator does not call undue attention to these otherwise puzzling references, but an attentive reader would realize that the difference in times would amount to a day upon the completion of the west-to-east circumnavigation of the globe.

Chapters 5-9

Once the journey begins, the novel digresses from the course of Fogg's travel. The narrator describes instead how Fogg's wager and his journey become a popular subject in the newspapers, leading to bookies taking wagers on whether he will succeed or not. However, all this comes to an end when Detective Fix, the police officer posted at Suez, Egypt, sends home (via telegraph) a request for a warrant to arrest Fogg on the suspicion that he is the robber of the Bank of England and that his journey and wager are an elaborate ruse to cover his escape. The narrative of the journey picks up at the Suez Canal, a vital link in the modern infrastructure that makes the journey possible, cutting several thousand miles off the route, which otherwise would have had to pass around Africa. Fix cannot receive his warrant in time, however, because Fogg is traveling at the maximum possible speed, so no courier carrying the document can hope to catch up with him. Consequently, Fix joins Fogg aboard his steamer and follows him on his course, hoping to find some way to delay him so that he can receive the written authority to make the arrest. In the meantime, Fix befriends Passepartout in order to pump him for information about Fogg, all of which he misinterprets to confirm his suspicions that Fogg is the thief.

Chapters 10-13

While Fogg is still aboard ship in the Indian Ocean he makes the acquaintance of Sir Francis Cromarty, an officer in the Indian Army with whom he begins to play whist. Once they reach Bombay, India, Fogg and his servant continue by train across the subcontinent, accompanied still by Sir Francis, who is going to join his regiment, and shadowed by Fix. They eventually discover that the rail connection has not, as reported, been completed yet and that they have to cross a mountain using local transport. Fogg buys an elephant at a ruinous price (calculating that he might have to spend as much as the twenty-thousand-pound wager to keep on schedule) and hires a local Parsee, or Parsi, *mahout* (elephant driver) to take them on to the railhead at Allahabad.

This route cuts through the lands of an independent Indian prince. There were several such rulers in British India who maintained essential autonomy within the British Raj. The territory is wild and overgrown with jungle, and the ruler still supports the ancient Hindu rite of *suttee*, whereby a widow throws herself onto her husband's funeral pyre. *Thugees* (bandits supposedly organized into a cultic association under the goddess Kali) are also still operating in the prince's lands. Reaching a site where a suttee will be taking place, Fogg learns from his mahout that the widow in question is the orphaned daughter of a wealthy Parsi family who was forced to marry an aged Hindu nobleman. Observing the preparations for the suttee from hiding, they see that she is no willing participant but will be thrown on the fire against her will. After trying throughout the night without success to find some way of rescuing the Parsi widow from her armed guards, Fogg is ready to simply rush them as she is placed on the fire, an action that would probably not only fail to save her but also get himself killed. This rash impulse redeems him in the eyes of Sir Francis, who wondered if the cold and mechanical Fogg was capable of human feeling. However, Passepartout instead simply leaps up onto the burning pyre and carries the girl off, making use of his circus and firefighting experience. The guards and priests are momentarily struck by superstitious fear, believing that Passepartout, who could not be seen clearly through the flames, was the dead husband come back to life, allowing Fogg and his companions, including the Parsi widow known as Mrs. Aouda, to escape.

Chapters 14-19

Fogg, Passepartout, and Mrs. Aouda continue by train, and Fogg promises to take the rescued woman to Hong Kong, where she believes a relative of hers lives. Once they reach Calcutta, Fix tries to delay them by encouraging prosecution of Passepartout for an earlier unwitting act of desecration. Fogg resolves this by posting and immediately forfeiting a two-thousand-pound bail, and they depart without further trouble. Aboard a ship for Singapore, Fogg and Mrs. Aouda begin their strange courtship, she acting with gratitude for his having saved her life, he acting with cold, calculating respect and exact correctness. The narrator describes the relations between them in terms of astronomical science, as if Mrs. Aouda is disturbing Fogg's orbit around the planet just as Neptune disturbs the orbit of Uranus, which allowed for the deduction of its existence before it was telescopically observed. After a brief stopover in Singapore, their ship steams on for Hong Kong. Passepartout encounters Fix again and forms the theory that he must be a private detective hired by Fogg's bettors at the Reform Club to monitor his progress.

In Hong Kong, Fogg learns that Mrs. Aouda's wealthy relative moved to Europe two years previously. Fogg then offers to conduct her to England. In an attempt to delay Fogg, Fix confesses his purpose to Passepartout, trying to enlist his aid but without success. Fix therefore separates Passepartout from his master and forces the two of them to make their way separately to Japan, with Fogg's trip on a privately chartered ship (on which he takes Mrs. Aouda and Fix, who still claims merely to be a fellow traveler) costing a fortune.

Chapters 20-24

Once in Yokohama, Japan, Passepartout decides that he must continue to press on along the route of Fogg's journey, in hopes of eventually meeting up with him. He happens to notice that a circus troupe is about to leave for San Francisco and joins them, on the basis of his experience as a circus acrobat. Participating in the troupe's final performance in Yokohama, Passepartout causes a human pyramid of acrobats to collapse when he spots Fogg in the audience and rushes out of his position to rejoin his master. Having learned that his servant had arrived on the scheduled steamer from Hong Kong, Fogg had set about looking for him, and "chance or a sort of premonition led him" to the circus.

The passage by steamship from Yokohama to San Francisco is uneventful, except in two respects. Fix's long-sought warrant had finally reached him in Japan, but it is now useless since they are outside of British territory. Fix thus determines that since Fogg evidently really does intend to return to England, all he can do is wait to arrest him there. Accordingly, he determines to now do everything he can to help speed Fogg toward British soil. He even convinces Passepartout of his intent to do this, discouraging the manservant from revealing Fix's true identity to Fogg. The other matter involves the narrator calling attention to the travelers' crossing of the international dateline in the middle of the Pacific Ocean on November 23. Passepartout notices that his watch again seems to agree with the ship's chronometers (when in fact it is exactly twelve hours off). Passepartout recalls Fix's earlier attempts to explain geography and time zones to him, producing a piece of comic diversion:

> "What a load of nonsense this scoundrel talked about the meridians,

the sun and the moon!" Passepartout repeated. "Huh! If people like that had their way we'd have some clever sorts of clocks and watches around! I knew for sure that one day or the other the sun would make up its mind to set itself by my watch."

Chapters 25-30

Once in San Francisco, Fogg and his companions are caught up in a riot that arises out of political campaigning. Fogg and Fix are personally assaulted by a ruffian named Colonel Stamp W. Proctor. Fogg resolves to return to America after completing his journey in order to fight a duel with this individual; as he cannot be detained by the matter just then, he and his companions board the train for New York. Passepartout discovers that Proctor is in fact also on the train, so he, Fix, and Mrs. Aouda try to prevent a meeting between the two men by keeping Fogg in his cabin playing whist. But the two inevitably meet and determine to fight for their honor. The railway employees and passengers obligingly put an entire car of the train at their disposal for this purpose, but just as they are pacing off for their duel, a Sioux war band attacks the train, and Fix and Proctor both turn their efforts to fighting the boarders. Since some Sioux warriors incapacitated the engineer and firemen, the train is running out of control at high speed. Passepartout saves the day, however, by using his acrobatic skills to crawl underneath the length of the train and decouple the cars from the engine, causing the train to come to rest just in front of a U.S. Army fort, whose soldiers drive off the attackers. Proctor is severely wounded in the attack, ending the matter of the duel. The Sioux, however, kidnaps some passengers, including Passepartout. Fogg goes with a troop of cavalry to rescue his servant, and he succeeds, but not before the train departs. When he returns, the narrator for the first time descriptively shows the growing affection between Fogg and Mrs. Aouda: "As for Mrs Aouda, she had taken the gentleman's hand and was squeezing it between her own, unable to speak."

Chapters 31-34

Fix finds a way for Fogg and his companions to continue, namely, by sailing over the frozen prairie on a sledge powered by sails like those on a racing yacht. In this way they proceed to Omaha, where they immediately board a train leaving for Chicago, to make a connection for New York. They arrive there, however, forty-five minutes after the steamer on which they have planned to sail left port. By his usual strategy of overpaying and bribery, of both the captain-owner and the crew, Fogg diverts a merchant ship bound for the French port of Bordeaux to Liverpool, England. However, the ship is not loaded with enough coal to cross the Atlantic Ocean at full steam the entire way, so Fogg is obliged to buy the ship from its captain for sixty thousand dollars and proceed to burn its wooden superstructure for fuel. This brings the total cost of the trip up to very nearly twenty thousand pounds, as Fogg had expected. But they only get as far as Ireland, where Fogg determines to take one of the fast sloops that carry mail from transatlantic steamers to Liverpool. Transferring to one of these, Fogg calculates, should give them sufficient time for him to win the wager.

As soon as they land in Liverpool, Fix finally arrests Fogg. Yet it turns out that the real thief was arrested three days previously in Scotland, which Fix, isolated aboard ship, had not known. The difficulties in getting Fogg released delay him just long enough to make returning to London to win the bet impossible. When Fogg steps out of his jail cell, he loses his temper for the only time in his life and strikes Fix down. Fogg's last effort of commissioning a special train makes no difference; the narrator assures the reader, "He had lost."

Chapters 35-37

Fogg returns to his house in Savile Row with Passepartout and Mrs. Aouda. His wager lost, the remainder of his fortune spent on the journey, Fogg is ruined, and his companions fear he might kill himself. Toward the evening of the next day, after Fogg has made an accounting of the few assets he has left, he meets with Mrs. Aouda, who surprises him by proposing marriage, which he can only accept.

With news of the real thief's capture, Fogg's wager became a popular item in the newspapers again, and public betting grew heavier than before. Naturally, there is a large crowd outside the Reform Club waiting for his return at the deadline of 8:45 p.m. on December 22. That very evening, while attempting to engage a priest to perform Fogg and Aouda's marriage, Passepartout discovers that the day Fogg thought was the twenty-third is really the twenty-second, as Fogg's calculation of the date was a day off. The wager began because so many newspaper and magazine articles had deduced from railway and steamship schedules that a journey around the world would take eighty days. While that might have been literally true in the sense of taking 1,920 hours, as far as the calendar was concerned the trip would take either seventy-nine (if traveling east-west) or eighty-one days (if traveling west-east) relative to the point of origin, because it would involve crossing the international dateline, which lies at 180 degrees longitude in the middle of the Pacific Ocean. Realizing that he has gained a day, Fogg proves able to go to the Reform Club and win his wager.

Characters

Mrs. Aouda

Mrs. Aouda is the daughter of a wealthy Parsi merchant whose death left her destitute, forcing her to marry a Hindu nobleman. As she is introduced into the story, he has just died, and she is in a drugged stupor about to be thrown onto her husband's funeral pyre against her will. Verne's initial description casts her as exotic—her garb is a rather fantastic version of traditional Hindu clothing —but is simultaneously meant to make her familiar to his readers, especially where she has "skin as white as a European's." Fogg's Parsi mahout adds more details of her life: "She was an Indian lady famous for her beauty, a Parsee by race and the daughter of a wealthy family of Bombay merchants. She had received a thoroughly English upbringing in the city and from her manners and schooling she could have been taken for a European." As the journey progresses Fogg takes her on to Hong Kong, where she believes she has a relative, but, since he has moved to Europe, Fogg resolves to take her to England with him. She is naturally grateful to Fogg for his role in saving her life and gradually finds herself falling in love with him, as she becomes impressed with his qualities of duty and honor and his ability to meet even the most difficult situations with effective action.

Brigadier General Sir Francis Cromarty

Sir Francis meets Fogg aboard ship between Suez and Bombay, and the two frequently play whist during the voyage. They continue to journey together on the trans-Indian railway since Sir Francis is going to join his regiment at Benares (modern Varanasi). He acts to a limited degree as a local guide to Fogg, advising him about how to negotiate the gap in the rail network and in the affair of rescuing Mrs. Aouda.

Inspector Detective Fix

Fix is dehumanized from the beginning by the fact that Verne never mentions his first name. The narrator's initial description marks Fix as unpleasant and deceptive: He is "a small, skinny man, quite intelligent-looking but nervous, with an almost-permanent frown on his face. His long eyelashes concealed a piercing gaze, but one that he could soften at will." He cannot arrest Fogg without a warrant from England, and since Fogg is traveling as fast as possible away from England, the warrant will never reach him; Fix therefore uses every kind of trickery he can devise to delay Fogg's journey. Probably this is the origin of his name, since "fix" can mean illicit interference in a sporting event or wager. During the second half of the journey, when it is in Fix's interest to speed Fogg along on his return to England so as to arrest him there, Fix seems to fall under the spell of Fogg's cold, calculating bravery and become a true follower of him in the same way as Passepartout and Mrs. Aouda. During the episode of Passepartout's kidnapping, Fix voluntarily stays behind to look after Mrs. Aouda. But when he imagines that Fogg is slipping out of his grasp, Fix reverts to his single-minded intent to arrest the suspect: "His true nature reasserted itself." He then does in fact arrest Fogg as soon as they return to England.

Phileas Fogg

Fogg is the central character of *Around the World in Eighty Days*. He undertakes the journey to which the title refers in order to resolve a wager about whether it is possible to complete such a trip or not. The name Phileas is an ancient Greek word meaning "beloved." Given the French custom of naming children for Christian saints, Verne most likely conceived of his character as named after St. Phileas, an Egyptian monk who was martyred during the persecution of the Roman emperor Maximian in 307. While the name is obscure in French, it is essentially nonexistent in English (perhaps the reason Verne chose it, as would be characteristic of his sense of humor), and it is sometimes replaced in translations and adaptations by "Phineas," an unusual but not unknown English name.

Verne initially describes his main character as "the enigmatic figure of Phileas Fogg, about whom nothing was known except that he was the most courteous of men and one of the most handsome gentlemen in English high society." Verne goes on to immediately inform the reader of a great deal about Fogg. He is a lawyer (and hence bears the title of esquire), though he does not practice law. He is tremendously rich, though he has no apparent business interests. He was admitted to the prestigious social circle of the Reform Club (whose members included many of the most important men in Britain) on his bankers' recommendation that a man of his wealth ought to belong. If he has family connections of any kind, no one knows anything about them. In fact, Fogg seems to have suddenly appeared in London society a few years before the novel opens in 1872 and to have done nothing except walk from his house to his club and back with the greatest regularity, following the same timetable each day, "with such mathematical precision that it fuelled other people's imagination." In addition, he seems to know more about geography than anyone else in London (though it could not be proved that he had ever traveled extensively); eventually he is able to navigate across the Atlantic. His only pastime is the card game of whist. He gambles on the game and most often wins, but he donates that money and much more to charity, playing rather to test his skill against that of his opponents.

In the second chapter Verne begins fleshing out his description of Fogg: "The gentleman gave the impression of something perfectly calibrated and finely balanced, like a chronometer made by a master craftsman." Throughout the novel, Fogg's virtues are always presented as mechanical or mathematical—virtues of the new age of progress through machinery, industry, and science. In contrast, Verne bestows on Fogg other characteristics meant to humanize him. For instance he gives his gambling winnings to charity, and on the night of his departure he gives twenty guineas— at least a thousand dollars today—to a woman begging on the street. His other selfless act is his rescue of Mrs. Aouda. In this case, while he says that he undertakes the effort only because he has the time, he is, before Passepartout's intervention, ready to throw his life away in a last-second vain effort to take her to safety. It is principally gratitude for her rescue that endears Fogg to Mrs. Aouda and leads to their eventual marriage. Fogg is presented as characteristically English in his sense of duty. He repeatedly, for instance, spends thousands of pounds to rescue Passepartout from some trouble or other he has gotten himself into, often at the risk of completing his journey on time, because he feels responsible for him.

Jean Passepartout

Passepartout is Fogg's manservant, newly hired at the outset of the novel. We do not know his actual surname, *passe-partout* being the French word for passport at the time, a nickname he says "I earned by my natural ability to get myself out of tricky situations." Because of the precise minute-by-minute schedule that Fogg insists Passepartout keep, we see the details of the job of the manservant in more detail than in most literature of that era. He had, for example, to awaken Fogg, prepare his breakfast, prepare his shaving equipment (including heating a bowl of water, since there was no hot tap water then), help him dress and prepare his hair, and so on, throughout the day. By way of a résumé, Passepartout tells Fogg about his work history, including stints as a circus acrobat and a fireman, foreshadowing his later exploits in the novel. As an ironic foreshadowing, he tells Fogg, "When I learnt that Mr Phileas Fogg was the most precise and most stay-at-home person in the United Kingdom, I came to sir's house in the hope of being able to lead a quiet life and put behind me everything associated with Passepartout, even the name."

Throughout the novel Passepartout's eyes, rather than Fogg's, are those of the tourist, taking in the local scenery for the reader. He also provides comic relief of a slapstick type. His work history, established in the first chapter, was contrived to uniquely suit him for each of the plot points that depend on him. Verne describes him as "a good chap with a friendly face and prominent lips that were made for eating, drinking and kissing." He is sensual and physical to the same degree that Fogg is cold and mechanical. He enjoys the local color, foodstuffs, and liquors that have no interest for his master. He is above all good natured and loyal to Fogg.

Colonel Stamp W. Proctor

This "enormous fellow with a red goatee beard, a ruddy complexion and broad shoulders" leads a gang that assaults Fogg's party during a political riot in San Francisco. Fogg determines to return after completing his journey to fight a duel with Proctor over the matter, but Proctor later encounters Fogg on the cross-country train and insults him again by belligerently taunting him about his judgment in playing whist. This leads to an immediate duel between the two; when it is broken up by a Sioux attack on the train, Proctor fights bravely and is severely wounded.

Themes

Tourism

The most obvious theme presented in *Around the World in Eighty Days* is travel. Indeed, the purpose of the novel is to demonstrate that travel of unprecedented scope and speed has become a reality, that anyone can travel within a few weeks to exotic places on the far side of the world that seem more like places of the imagination. Progress has allowed fantasies of faraway cities to be replaced by real experience. Verne treats Fogg's fantastic journey from an experiential viewpoint as an ordinary tourist trip. This supports the idea that human progress is making the world smaller and safer—indeed, is conquering it. But Verne did not base Fogg's travels on his own experience. Many local details of the novel's various episodes, and especially Verne's minute concentration on the transportation network, were probably based on another nineteenth-century genre of travel writing, the touristic handbook such as the Baedeker's. This series of red handbooks, familiar to every traveler in the nineteenth and early twentieth centuries, included a separate volume for every destination of any importance throughout Europe, North America, and most of Africa and Asia. They provided not only detailed information on railway and maritime transportation but also lists of hotels and restaurants, complete with menus and prices, as well as detailed descriptions of local attractions. A man like Phileas Fogg, who was never known to have traveled, could thus have nevertheless gained the highly detailed knowledge of geography he was famous for in the Reform Club simply by reading these guidebooks. Verne most likely followed the same procedure to learn the details central to his travel novel, which in most other works of fiction would have served as mere background.

The Baedeker's handbooks certainly provided the kind of colorful details with which Verne ornaments *Around the World in Eighty Days*. Verne's narrative moves from point to point around the globe: "Paris, Brindisi, Suez, Bombay, Calcutta, Singapore, Hong Kong, Yokohama, San Francisco, New York, Liverpool and London." In just the same way one could leap from volume to volume in a library of Baedeker's guides, such as might be owned by a gentleman's club. (Oddly, for eastern North America, where Verne had travelled personally, all local details are absent from the narrative.) The encounter with India in the novel, for instance, begins with precise statements of its area in square miles and its population. Next comes a precise description of the main rail lines with the mountains they pass over and the principal stops. Bombay consists of points of touristic interest: libraries, marketplaces, the seat of government, mosques, churches, temples, synagogues, and the local ancient ruins. The local ethnic cuisine is sampled, and local color is described: a Parsi festival featuring Indian dancing girls. Passepartout gets into trouble because he enters an Indian temple for purely touristic enjoyment, without removing his shoes first—precisely the kind of customary detail he could have read in a Baedeker's if he had taken the time to do so. To advance to the next destination, Verne faithfully follows the map of the railway lines and describes the type of train in service on them. He proceeds in the same manner for each stop and each leg of the journey, thus giving a grand summary of the nineteenth-century tourist experience.

Topics for Further Study

- Paul Theroux is a great American travel writer. Read any of his travel books, such as *The Great Railway Bazaar*, *The Old Patagonian Express*, or *Dark Star Safari*, and give a presentation to your class comparing his experiences in the late twentieth century to those of

Fogg and Passepartout in *Around the World in Eighty Days.*

- Prepare a map showing the route of Fogg's journey around the world with small illustrations of interesting scenes from the novel at the places on the map where they happened.

- *Around the World in Eighty Days* celebrates a vision of unlimited progress, the idea that the world has become better and will only continue to become better through the advancement of technology. Has the history of the twentieth century borne out this proposition? Or has technology caused more problems than it has solved? Organize a class debate on this question.

- Watch the 1956 film version of *Around the World in Eighty Days.* Then prepare a class presentation on the similarities to and differences from the novel. Be sure to show clips from the film that illustrate your points.

Science and Technology

Verne is generally, if somewhat simplistically, known as a science fiction writer, so it is no surprise that science plays a large part in *Around the World in Eighty Days*. Perhaps the main theme of the work is that the technology created by modern science is completely transforming the world, most notably making transportation many orders of magnitude faster and more dependable and making the extraordinary journey of the work's title possible. Not merely is the world being changed, but furthermore its change is heading, like Fogg, on a definite path at the highest possible speed toward a final goal, scientific utopia. All of the technological advances that represented progress in the nineteenth century were tied together in travel. The steam engine, iron rails, and steam-powered steel-hulled ships combined to represent the highest point of industrialism. The transportation network itself had become global in scale, providing the main elements of the novel's plot as well as its title. Moreover, unlike, for instance, the equally rapid advances being made in the sophistication of military weapons, transportation and travel were viewed as an unalloyed good for common people that would serve to link the world together. Fogg symbolizes the new modern man who is shaped by science and the new technology; while not lacking in human virtues, he acts with the efficiency of a machine, and even his innermost emotions, such as with his falling in love with Mrs. Aouda, are described in metaphors based on the science of celestial mechanics.

Verne reveals a number of aspects of nineteenth-century progress in the novel, through both the story and his telling of it. The unification of the world through travel was being accomplished in one particular way, colonialism, by which the rest of the world was being linked to Europe and made over in Europe's image. Civilization was proving triumphant and would tame the rest of the world. Thus in India Fogg passes through the city of Monghyr, an industrial center that is like the British cities of Manchester or Birmingham transported to the East. The native peoples are judged according to pseudoscientific racial categories popularly accepted in the nineteenth century. Mrs. Aouda is the most acceptable non-European because of her constantly mentioned whiteness, in contrast to the natives of the Andaman Islands (between India and Southeast Asia): "The savage inhabitants of the island … stand at the very bottom of the human scale." Far from being a visionary, Verne was as locked into the popular beliefs and traditions of his time as anyone else, and *Around the World in Eighty Days* reflects the science and beliefs of that time.

Style

Orientalism

Orientalism in one of its senses is a constructed way of viewing cultures outside of Europe or the United States connected to the political and economic relationships of colonialism that dominated interactions between the West and the rest of the world in the nineteenth century. Orientalism denies the real identities of African, Asian, or American Indian cultures and recasts them as an exotic, romantic "other." Many of Verne's novels take place in exotic settings and exhibit an orientalist attitude toward the strange and foreign, treating it as a mysterious and exotic departure from the everyday world of the European reader while at the same time making the setting comprehensible by using the familiar stereotypes by which the reading public comprehends the exotic.

To a large extent the crux of *Around the World in Eighty Days* is the railway spanning the Indian Subcontinent, the report on the completion of which impels Fogg on his journey and the unreality of which presents the chief obstacle to his journey. In the space between the two rail heads in India, Fogg and his companions plunge into a fictitious, romantic world. It is a world different than the one reported in the newspapers and so to Fogg a world that is unreal. Given that railroads tend to follow roads, it is unlikely that such a gap would have been crossed by any means other that a horse-drawn wagon or coach, but Fogg rides an elephant, perhaps because that is a popular cliché the reading public would have had about "exotic" India. The adventure he has in this fictive space involves the cult of the *thugees* and the rite of *suttee*, both elements of Indian culture that the British had, by and large, suppressed by 1872. The *thugees* were an organized system of criminal gangs that robbed and murdered travelers and looked to the Hindu goddess Kali to protect them in their dangerous work. But Verne adopts a more fantastic and romantic interpretation of their activities well known from the popular press, that their murders were a cultic act of worship to Kali. The suttee, in turn, was the Hindu custom of a widow committing suicide by throwing herself onto the funeral pyre of her husband as a final act of devotion. Verne heightens the dramatic sense of the act by presenting not a Hindu but a Parsi woman (Mrs. Aouda) forced to undergo this ritual against her will but rescued at the last moment. In fact, the suttee and the thugees existed (albeit a half century or so before Verne's novel is set) at opposite ends of the social structure of Indian society, yet Verne chooses to tie them together, making the thugees responsible for carrying out the suttee of their victim. There is nothing to truly connect them in reality except their alien and romantic character.

The setting of this portion of the novel is the last mountain fastness of fanatical Hinduism where the British have not established their authority (which, seemingly improbably, is nevertheless the area where the British are building the unifying link in the Indian rail network), surrounded by jungle inhabited by cheetahs, leopards, and other "flesh-eating animals," and where Fogg eats a meal of bananas, a fruit then wholly unknown in Europe. The suttee is to be carried out by "a group of elderly fakirs ... working themselves up into a furious frenzy. Their bodies were streaked with bright yellow markings and covered with cross-shaped incisions from which blood was oozing.... Behind them [were] a few Hindu priests, in the full splendour of their oriental costumes." Although used here to represent the epitome of "otherness," the image seems to be drawn from the Hebrew Bible (1 Kings 18), a founding document of Western culture, with its prophets of Baal, who induced religious ecstasy in themselves by cutting their skin with knives. Verne is thus drawing on stereotypical images of the other rather than describing real Indian institutions. Mrs. Aouda, on the other hand, forms a link between this exotic world and the West. Fogg and his companions rescue her from the depths of the Orient. She is an Indian, but a Parsi, a member of a monotheistic religion like Christianity or Judaism. She is also described as being European in appearance, that is, "white," and educated so that she speaks and acts like an aristocratic British woman. She forms the link to the oriental world that Fogg is able to take with him back to Britain and eventually join with in marriage. In this way Fogg overcomes the other and makes it Western, thus fulfilling the positive self-perception of colonialism in replacing exotic culture with European culture.

Encyclopedic Literature

Verne's publisher Hetzel insisted that Verne's volumes in the Extraordinary Voyages series contain a large amount of educational material about the newly burgeoning Victorian science and technology as a selling point to persuade parents to buy the books for their children. The idea was that reading these books would help prepare children for the technical professions of the future unfamiliar to the parents. On the other hand, Verne himself had not done much traveling outside of western Europe and the eastern United States. Both of these factors conditioned the nearly wholesale incorporation into *Around the World in Eighty Days* and his other novels of material closely based on almanacs, encyclopedias, and other reference works. *Around the World in Eighty Days* contains countless passages that Verne appears to have adapted from such technical literature with very little alteration. This is evident, for instance, in his comments on naval architecture:

> The ships of the P&O line which sail the China Seas have a serious design fault. The ratio between their draught when laden and their depth has been wrongly calculated and as a result they lack stability in heavy seas.... These ships are therefore far inferior

—if not by their engines and their steam apparatus, then at least in their design—to the sorts of ships used by the French mail service, such as the *Impératrice* and the *Cambodge*. Whereas, according to the engineers' calculations, the latter can take on board a weight of water equal to their own weight before sinking, the P&O ships, the *Golconda*, the *Korea* and lastly the *Rangoon*, could not take on board a sixth of their weight without going down.

These details must have come from reading of the technical literature produced by the various firms involved. Another kind of literature, perhaps a travel book, would have supplied this kind of detail, explaining the geography and limnology of the great Salt Lake in Utah:

The Great Salt Lake, which is about seventy miles long and thirty-five miles wide, is situated at about 3,800 feet above sea level.... It has a high salt content, since its waters hold in solution a quarter of their weight in solid matter. Its specific gravity is 1,170 compared to 1,000 for distilled water.... However, the idea that the density of its waters is too great for anyone to dive into it is untrue.

In this way Verne's writing contains many qualities of a compilation or anthology of technical and scientific literature, which in his era formed popular subjects of fascination in the way that computer science does in contemporary literature, as for instance in the novels of Michael Crichton or William Gibson.

Mass-Market Publishing

Verne was part of one of the earliest mass-market publishing empires, that of Pierre-Jules Hetzel (1814-1886). Hetzel in some measure created Verne's phenomenal publishing success through the integrated use of magazine, newspaper, and book publishing. He created an entire series of Verne's books, titled "Voyages extraordinaires" ("Extraordinary Voyages"), in order to promote completist collecting. Verne's novels were regularly serialized in a newspaper or magazine owned by Hetzel and then published in book form at the end of the year, making them available as Christmas presents. Each book was published simultaneously in three different formats with three different prices, ranging from cheap paperbacks to elaborately illustrated hardbacks.

Around the World in Eighty Days was the single greatest success in this series, especially for Verne. In addition to his usual collaboration with Hetzel, Verne coauthored a highly successful and long-running play that relied on elaborate special effects to simulate the exotic events of the novel, such as the burning pyre from which Passepartout rescues Mrs. Aouda, as well as the motion of the various trains and ships that figure so largely in the story. Verne personally made more money from this stage enterprise than he did from almost all his book royalties combined; it was in some sense the nineteenth-century equivalent of selling film rights. Most of the transportation firms mentioned in the books were real companies. As the serialized chapters became more and more popular (a process reflected, or predicted, in the novel itself as newspaper readers in England become more and more interested in Fogg's wager and journey), several railroad and steamship companies offered to pay Verne to make sure their services were mentioned by name. Verne claimed that as a gentleman he had to turn down such offers, but whether this is true or not, it was perhaps the earliest demonstration of the principle of product placement, the now ubiquitous practice by which companies pay to have their products featured in popular narratives.

Compare & Contrast

- **1872:** Verne's novel *Around the World in Eighty Days* suggests that a journey around the world using regularly scheduled commercial transportation (railroads and steamships) can be accomplished in eighty days. Fifteen years later, the American journalist Nellie Bly beats Verne's fictional record, traveling the world in just over seventy-two days.

Today: A journey around the world using regularly scheduled commercial transportation (airliners) would take as little as forty-five hours.

- **1872:** The Parsi community in India is open in its embrace of British culture, expanding demographically, financially, and culturally.

Today: The Parsi community is shrinking, with one of the lowest birth rates in the world, and is deeply divided between members who wish to preserve old conservative traditions and others who are leaving the community through intermarriage with other groups.

- **1872:** Steam and steel technology symbolize the cutting edge of human progress.

Today: In the popular imagination, computer technology now symbolizes human progress.

Parsis and Westernization

Mrs. Aouda, the woman that Fogg and his companions rescue from the *suttee* (the ritual of a Hindu wife burning herself to death on her husband's funeral pyre), is a Parsi. The Parsis (now less commonly spelled "Parsees") are the descendants of Iranians who fled their homeland in the eighth to tenth centuries in the face of the Arab conquest. A main reason that they fled was to preserve their traditional religion rather than convert to Islam. Their religion was Zoroastrianism, named after their prophet Zoroaster, who lived in the mid-second millennium BCE. He was the first prophetic figure to found an entirely new religion, preaching that his followers should worship God (Ahura Mazda in the Iranian language) and his semidivine helpers while fighting against the evil principle that exists in the world (Angra Mainyu or Ahriman). History, in the Parsi view, is leading to a definite end when Zoroaster will be reborn and herald the final victory of God over evil together with the dissolution of the physical world and the judgment of the dead as to whether they had followed God or the evil principle.

By the nineteenth century, the Parsi population in India was concentrated in Bombay (modern Mumbai), where they formed a large and prosperous mercantile middle class, amounting to more than 100,000 people, or a fifth of the city's population. Because it brought tremendous advantages in business, the Parsis rapidly adopted British-style education and produced a disproportionate number of leading Indian physicians, lawyers, teachers, journalists, and other professionals, as well as businessmen. Praising them for their adoption of modernity, Verne states that the Parsis are "the most hard-working, civilized, intelligent and austere of the Indians and are the race to which the wealthy native merchants of Bombay currently belong." By the mid-1850s, upper-class Parsi girls were also beginning to receive Western educations (at least through a grammar-school or high-school level), which helps explain Aouda's degree of anglicization and easy interaction with her British rescuer and eventual husband. Despite any religious scruples, Parsis also formed an extensive trading community throughout the British Empire, and Fogg and his companions begin to encounter them as far west as Aden, in Arabia.

Parsis had to overcome their own particular obstacles to accommodate their integration with the modern world. Like Jews, they were hampered in this by purity laws that had functioned adequately in the tribal existence of their ancestors thousands of years ago but which made interaction with the modern world difficult. In particular, Parsis considered fire to be a sacred manifestation of God on earth and maintained perpetually burning fires in their temples; they considered the harnessing of fire for any purpose (such as warfare) other than cooking or illumination to be blasphemous. For this reason, the steam engine was viewed as unclean and something that Parsis could not come into contact with. As a result, Parsis, again like Jews, split into traditionalist and reforming factions. At the same time, educated Parsis became leaders in the scientific study of their own religious literature (the Avesta, attributed to Zoroaster, and a few later works). The conflict between tradition and modernity in regard to the Parsi religion led to the doctrine that a separate tradition taught by "secret masters" revealed that in fact nothing in the Avesta was incompatible with modernity. The interaction of Parsis holding such beliefs with Western occultists helped lead to the formation of interfaith spirituality known today in the United States and Europe as "New Age." The deep Parsi religious belief that the purpose of human existence is to fight evil was put into action in the nineteenth century by a number of charitable organizations funded by wealthy Parsis, providing a complete social safety net of subsistence, medical care, and education for even the poorest members of the Parsi community. Accordingly, Verne's narrative condition that Aouda, though the daughter of a wealthy Bombay Parsi merchant, was abandoned by the community when she was orphaned and forced to marry a Hindu prince is far-fetched as a historical probability.

Critical Overview

Verne has enjoyed a renaissance in the opinion of French critics in the last generation, but in the English-speaking world he is still often not taken as a serious author. In fact, Verne is often classed as children's literature. It is true that Hetzel serialized many of Verne's most strongly scientific pieces in his magazines intended for juvenile audiences because those stories were in part considered didactic, that is, teaching about science. However, Verne did not aim his work at children, nor were they mainly taken as such in France. Verne's reputation as a juvenile author in the English-speaking world depends mainly on the purposes and faults of his translators. Translations (frequently anonymous) of Verne are often made explicitly for children, and in those cases the text is likely to be either summarized or radically altered, ironically leaving out the most scientific and technical elements of the books. *Around the World in Eighty Days* is certainly not children's literature, but it has suffered from misdirected marketing to younger audiences often enough. A notable example is the 2004 Disney film adaptation of the story, which was heavily marketed to children, abandoned any effort at scientific or dramatic plausibility, and seemed to take place in some sort of steam-punk fantasy world rather than the reality of 1872 where Verne set his book.

A reappraisal of Verne's oeuvre began in the

1960s among French critics and has slowly made its way into the English-speaking world. Arthur B. Evans's seminal (for English criticism of Verne) *Jules Verne Rediscovered: Didacticism and the Scientific Novel* points out that what is often misunderstood as science fiction in Verne is his praise of the positivist tendency in nineteenth-century thought and its extrapolation. This positivism is apparent in the scrupulously realist *Around the World in Eighty Days* in that the speed of modern transportation seems, in the book's ending, to even create time itself. Evans points out that Verne's writing style, especially in the presentation of human character, is "consistently condemned by critics as 'superficial,' 'wooden,' and 'nonliterary.'" And this is nowhere more true than in the flat characterizations spelled out at the beginning of the novel for Fogg and Passepartout. But Evans defends Verne's stylistic choice on the ground that it is modeled on the presentation of facts in scientific literature. Communicated by Andrew Martin in *The Knowledge of Ignorance: From Genesis to Jules Verne* is the basic insight of French scholarship that Verne is a champion of the shift from the biblical paradigm, wherein knowledge led to humanity's fall in the garden of Eden, to a modern paradigm wherein knowledge for its own sake brings salvation; in Verne's literature, logic and engineering replace lyricism.

William Butcher has done the most of any scholar writing in English to provide a context for *Around the World in Eighty Days* based on the new wave of French Verne scholarship. In the introduction to his translation of the work, he characterizes its author as highly experimental and far ahead of his time. Butcher finds Verne's overarching themes in the novel to be space and time themselves. He sees the leap in the narrative from Paris to Suez to be an internalization in Verne's style of the instantaneous communication made possible by the telegraph. Butcher praises the ending of the novel, which symmetrically returns to its origin in the Reform Club via flashback cut off by Fogg's entry as an unexpected *deus ex machina* (literally, "a god from a machine," a character or device introduced to resolve a plot that otherwise cannot be resolved) to win the bet. Finally, Butcher argues that the narrator of the book is highly unusual because he seems to labor under many of the misapprehensions of the characters: the narrator informs the reader, inaccurately, that the railway crossing India has been completed, that the image of Passepartout rescuing Mrs. Aouda from the burning pyre is the dead Indian prince come back to life, and that the wager has been lost. For Butcher, this makes the novel uniquely modern in that the reader can find no definite framework of truth.

Among other studies of Verne, Timothy Unwin, in his *Verne: "Le tour du monde en quatre-vingts jours"* (which uses the original French in its title but which is written in English), follows in Butcher's footsteps, drawing on French scholarship to situate *Around the World in Eighty Days* as a link between traditional linear novels and modern works of introspection and experimentation. Curiously, even Verne scholars can show a lack of familiarity with *Around the World in Eighty Days.* For instance, in *Jules Verne: An Exploratory Biography,* Herbert R. Lottman refers to Mrs. Aouda as being Hindu.

What Do I Read Next?

- *The Jules Verne Encyclopedia,* by Brian Taves and Stephen Michaluk, Jr. (1996), provides a wide variety of information, focusing on the history of publication, translations, and adaptations of Verne's works.

- The Web site of Zvi Har'El's Jules Verne Collection (http://jv.gilead.org.il) provides a wide spectrum of resources, including online texts of Verne's works, scans of the original illustrations of many of Verne's books, scholarly articles about

Verne, a discussion forum, and much more.

- Emmanuel J. Mikel's 1991 translation of *Twenty Thousand Leagues under the Sea* (1869-70) presents a full and careful rendition of Verne's second best-known novel, complete with introduction and notes.

- *Paris in the Twentieth Century* was Verne's second novel, written in 1863 but rejected by his publisher Hetzel and so not published until 1994. Translated by Richard Howard in 1996, the work presents a grim dystopian future where technology has destroyed traditional culture and suggests an entirely different path that Verne might have taken without Hetzel's guidance.

- H. G. Wells was in some sense Verne's rival as a "science fiction" author, though Verne disliked the comparison since he saw himself dealing with scientific reality while Wells pursued more fantastic subjects. The original 1898 text of Wells's famous *War of the Worlds* was edited and annotated by Leon Stover in 2001.

Sources

Boyce, Mary, *Zoroastrians: Their Religious Beliefs and Practices*, Routledge & Kegan Paul, 1985, pp. 196-215.

Burton, Richard Francis, *Of No Country: An Anthology of the Works of Sir Richard Burton*, edited by Frank McLynn, Scribner, 1990.

Bury, J. B., *The Idea of Progress: An Inquiry into Its Origin and Growth*, Macmillan, 1920, pp. vii-xi, 316, 330.

Butcher, William, "Introduction," in *Around the World in Eighty Days*, translated by William Butcher, Oxford University Press, 2008, pp. vii-xxxi.

Evans, Arthur B., *Jules Verne Rediscovered: Didacticism and the Scientific Novel*, Greenwood Press, 1988, p. 54.

Gallagher, Edward J., Judith A. Mistichelli, and John A. Van Eerde, *Jules Verne: A Primary and Secondary Bibliography*, G. K. Hall, 1980.

Keynes, John Maynard, *The Economic Consequences of the Peace*, Harcourt, Brace and Howe, 1920, pp. 9-12.

Lottman, Herbert R., *Jules Verne: An Exploratory Biography*, St. Martin's Press, 1996, pp. 162-64.

Martin, Andrew, *The Knowledge of Ignorance: From Genesis to Jules Verne*, Cambridge University

Press, 1985.

Rivers, Christopher, *Face Value: Physiognomical Thought and the Legible Body in Marivaux, Lavater, Balzac, Gautier, and Zola*, University of Wisconsin Press, 1994.

Said, Edward, *Culture and Imperialism*, Vintage Books, 1994, pp. 93-116.

Swedin, Eric G., and David L. Ferro, *Computers: The Life Story of a Technology*, Greenwood Press, 2005, pp. 1-24.

Unwin, Timothy, *Verne: "Le tour du monde en quatre-vingts jours,"* University of Glasgow, 1992.

Verne, Jules, *Around the World in Eighty Days*, translated by Michael Glencross, Penguin, 2004.

Further Reading

Bly, Nellie, *Around the World in Seventy-Two Days*, Pictorial Weeklies, 1890.

> This book by the pioneering female reporter Nellie Bly capitalized on the popularity of Verne's novel. Her articles about her real travels in 1889 were also published in newspapers and then collected in book form. The text of the book is available online at http://digital.library.upenn.edu/women/bly/w through the digital library at the University of Pennsylvania.

Butcher, William, *Verne's Journey to the Centre of the Self: Space and Time in the Voyages Extraordinaires*, St. Martin's Press, 1991.

> This is a seminal English-language critical study of Verne's oeuvre as a whole.

Gildea, Robert, *Children of the Revolution: The French, 1799-1914*, Harvard University Press, 2008.

> This is a recent standard survey of French history and culture covering the entirety of Verne's lifetime. It provides a useful background for understanding Verne within his own society.

Hinnells, John R., *Persian Mythology*, Hamlyn, 1973.

> This work, intended in part for younger readers, gives a basic introduction to the beliefs and history of the Parsi religion.